Thinking with a Line (TWAL©)

Smith College Campus School

Thinking with a Line (TWAL©)

Teacher's Guide to the Interactive CD-ROM

Cathy Weisman Topal

Davis Publications, Inc.
Worcester, Massachusetts

Copyright © 2005
Davis Publications, Inc.
Worcester, Massachusetts

ISBN: 0-87192-714-4

Library of Congress Control Number: 2005925632

10 9 8 7 6 5 4 3 2 1

Printed in the United States of America

For my colleagues at the Center for Early Childhood Education at Smith College and the Smith College Campus School. It has been an honor and a pleasure to explore and document the power and potential of materials with you and the children over these many years.

Contents

Contents

Preface

As a teacher of visual arts at the pre-K through elementary school level and an instructor of visual arts education at the college level, my passion for using materials and seeing their potential as languages for learning only grows.

The delicate, interactive process of offering a material or tool, listening and observing as children explore, and reacting in ways that support their discoveries fascinates me, both as a teacher and a researcher. I've been working with children and printmaking for over twenty years, using a variety of different processes and printing materials. In the past few years, I've been keeping track of the amazing constructions that children have been able to create by printing with a single line.

This program grew from experimenting with one line in its simplest form. By experimenting with many groups of children of different ages, I began to see what they could do with a printed line, and noted areas of interest that now form the sections of this program. Children discover that they can construct a variety of lines and shapes and combine them to create complex structures such as letters, buildings, machines, and vehicles. They also begin to create structures found in nature such as snowflakes, skeletons, and the branching patterns of trees.

Since developing an understanding of spatial orientation is basic to all of this work, line printing is a way to help children with basic visual literacy and the mechanics of writing. Once children figure out and construct a structure, they intuitively understand with their hands and eyes and minds how to approach and improve their drawing or painting or writing of that construction. Their interest and attention spans lengthen as they become invested in perfecting their constructions.

The principles of the Reggio Emilia approach to education have inspired many of the ideas behind *Thinking with a Line*. I am grateful to the educators with whom I have studied this approach. My thinking has also been influenced by the work of Rudolph Arnheim, Friedrich Froebel, Howard Gardner, Elliot W. Eisner, and Rhoda Kellogg. A collaboration with the technology department, supported by the Dean's Academic Support Fund and The Center for Foreign Languages and Cultures at Smith College made this exciting, interactive program possible.

Thinking with a Line gives teachers and children many ways to meet the National Visual Arts Standards as well as national standards in mathematics, science, and English language arts. Applicable standards are listed in the appendix to this guide, along with the chapters that support them.

Please visit the companion Web site <www.smith.edu/twal> for more information on the philosophies behind the creation of *Thinking with a Line*.

Thinking with a Line (TWAL©)

Introduction

The *Thinking with a Line* CD-ROM and this Teacher's Guide give you the background and preparation you need to teach your students how to think and create with a line. It is an exciting, easy-to-use art and visual literacy tool that will help you to cultivate the craft of teaching with studio art materials.

The CD-ROM

Thinking with a Line is an interactive computer program. The CD-ROM contains Part 1, "Thinking with a Line," and Part 2, "Creating with a Line." The "pages" of the CD look like they would in a book. But there is a difference. Many of the images are actually short video clips that highlight teachers and children at key moments of teaching and learning. Both video and audio clips suggest ways to set up, introduce, and extend a variety of projects about line—the most basic of all the art elements and a vital reading-readiness, writing, and construction tool. The twelve chapters in the Teacher's Guide, and a great many more activities, come alive on the CD-ROM. Use the CD to

- see an overview of the entire program
- watch video clips of teacher demonstrations
- observe children at key moments of discovery and learning
- study examples of children's strategies, solutions, and comments
- listen to important teaching tips
- learn ways to expand a lesson
- see other lesson plans and project ideas under each topic
- discover related projects that introduce other studio art materials

▶ video Watch a video of a five-year-old explaining her creation.

The CD-ROM is rich with colorful, beautiful works of art by children, artists, architects, and craftspeople from many times and cultures.

The Teacher's Guide

The Teacher's Guide contains twelve chapters that correspond to the sections of the CD-ROM. Although many more ideas are contained on the CD, the Teacher's Guide is intended for use as a handy reference in the classroom. Each of the twelve chapters includes:

- a rationale and introduction to use as starters so that you can integrate learning with your classroom goals

- motivating strategies for introducing an investigation
- key questions to provoke thinking and curiosity
- directions in stages so that you can easily guide and build upon children's work as you see it developing
- activities to extend each exploration
- follow-up ideas
- important teaching tips highlighted with an asterisk
- a list of additional ideas and projects that can be found on the CD
- a list of suggested children's books to use with each project

Why Line?

Lines give you information—just like words—and it is easy to read their language. Line is the most basic of all the art elements and is a key to unlocking the creative process.

Identifying and following vertical, horizontal, diagonal, and other kinds of lines helps us see and understand how shapes, letters, designs, and buildings are constructed—and gives us the tools we need to form our own constructions.

As explored in Part 1 of this book, "Thinking with a Line," a line becomes a tool for thinking when it is used to discover the beginnings of writing, reading, mathematics, and design.

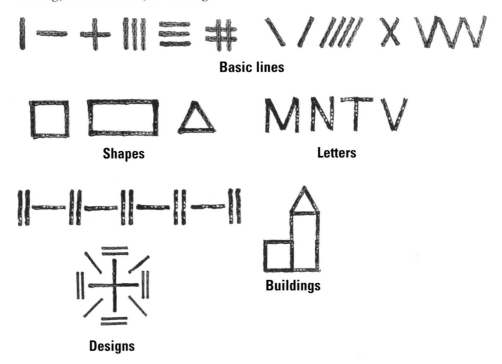

Basic lines

Shapes

Letters

Designs

Buildings

Part 2, "Creating with a Line," builds upon the explorations of Part 1. In the seven chapters in Part 2, children identify and print vertical, horizontal, diagonal, and curved lines to explore

1. composition in works of art
2. design of signs and posters
3. the crystalline structure of snowflakes
4. the human skeleton
5. trees and branching structures in nature
6. architecture
7. how simple machines combine to form complex machines

Composition

Signs and posters

Snowflakes

Branching

Architecture

Skeletons

Machines

What Is Line Printing?

Line printing is a process for creating lines. Part 1, "Thinking with a Line," gives children step-by-step instructions on how to turn a small rectangle of cardboard dipped into paint into a tool for making lines.

Dip into paint.   Press firmly onto paper.   Lift.   Repeat.

By repeating a single line, children discover they can print vertical, horizontal, and diagonal lines. They also discover ways to extend, cross, and space their lines. They find that when lines connect they can form shapes and a multitude of other structures. Through practice, children learn how many strong lines they can print before they have to dip into the paint again.

Lena, age five, uses a piece of cardboard as a tool for thinking and creating. The printing process enables her to repeat and vary her lines.

By combining lines and shapes, children begin creating complex structures such as letters, alphabets, patterns and designs, trees and plants, buildings, boats, machines, and vehicles. Even young children begin to construct with intention. Projects and themes emerge naturally, and teachers recognize how the skills developed here can enhance curriculum goals in many subject areas. Working out ideas and theories with studio projects at the same time that you are investigating curriculum concepts engages children's multiple intelligences.

Why Line Printing?

Children using the process of line printing often form constructions that they might not be able to draw or write, or might not consider drawing or writing. Children just entering the stage of representational drawing, or having difficulty drawing, sometimes make a huge leap when offered line printing as a tool for composing pictures, letters, and designs.

Children who are struggling to develop fine motor skills will find a new, fluent means of expression and a tool for constructing knowledge. Although it may be difficult for children to draw straight lines, they can easily master the process of line printing. The ability to make a series of marks and control their placement requires visual, motor, and thinking skills. This ability both precedes and is essential to drawing and writing and develops the skills needed to recognize letters and to read.

Adding a Curved Line

Expanding from straight lines to a curved line makes it easy to create curved shapes and letters and add domes and arches to buildings, bridges, and other structures.

The insides of masking tape rolls or the edges of paper or Styrofoam cups cut in half make excellent printing tools for creating curved lines.

Hold the half circle on its edge. Place carefully so as not to smear. Lift straight up.

Jon, age seven, demonstrates printing a curved line.

Connecting Line Printing to the Curriculum

Teachers of children in enrichment and after-school programs will find that the content areas in Part 2, "Creating with a Line," offer interesting ways to make learning appealing and challenging. Line printing helps children construct their understandings about the human skeleton, architecture, the hexagonal structure of snowflakes, elements of an effective sign or poster, and much more. Line printing experiences provide opportunities for children to build confidence in their creative abilities.

"If I can do it, you can do it," says Marcus, age eight.

Supplies and Processes

Line printing supplies are simple, low cost, and are probably already in your classroom. Cardboard is the most common printing tool and is used in all of the activities in this book. As you discover the many applications of Thinking with a Line, *you will begin to save cardboard boxes and cut them into line printing stamps.*

This section is filled with commonsense ideas and tips for how to effectively use and manage studio materials in a classroom. It is helpful to read before you begin.

Print with the side you can look through.

Supplies

- 3" x 2½" rectangles of corrugated cardboard cut on a paper cutter, 2 per child
- squeeze bottles of poster paint
- Styrofoam trays or paper plates for holding paint
- paper
  - 9" x 12" newsprint for practice work
  - 12" x 18" newsprint and white paper for most practicing and printing
  - 18" x 24" newsprint or white paper for larger work and final prints
  - 12" x 18" Fadeless™ or construction paper
  - large rolls of paper for group murals
  - newspaper for covering tables and padding the work surface

Paper size will depend on your circumstances and on the size of your work area.

Keep supplies simple and basic. One color of poster paint is all that you need for most activities. Using a squeeze bottle makes the paint easy to distribute. Limiting choices to one line and one color at the beginning puts the emphasis on placement and construction.

Other Line Printing Tools

After children have become proficient with the process of line printing and have created their beginning structures, they might need more line options. Introduce one tool at a time—especially with younger children.

The sizes of the tools are proportionate. The big cardboard is 3" x 2½". The small cardboard is 1½" x 2½".

Cut the inside of a masking tape roll in half to create a 3-inch curve. Paper and Styrofoam cups cut in half also make excellent tools for printing large curved lines.

Save empty masking tape rolls and ask others to save them as well. The large curves are more difficult to collect, so don't throw them away after printing. Let them dry out and reuse them.

Cut toilet paper rolls in half and then in half again to create the small curves. Make sure children use the flat side for printing.

The way in which a new tool is offered makes a big difference in how it is received. Make the addition of a new tool special and invite discussion about the possibilities opened up by this new kind of line.

✱ The most common mistake I have made is to offer too many materials too fast. As a general rule of thumb, begin with the large line tool and encourage exploration and exchange of ideas. At the same time, be prepared with additional tools and materials to offer when you wish to extend and deepen an exploration.

Found Objects

Found objects are exciting and suggestive when added to linear constructions. Small found objects that print clear lines and shapes work best.

Be on the lookout for small bottle caps, spools, pencil grips, and other objects that hold potential for printing. You will be surprised by what you discover!

Give just one object to each child. When children have only one object, they figure out how to use it in many different ways. They can always exchange objects with a friend.

Three-year-olds explore objects that print different kinds and sizes of circles. Working with materials is also a social activity. Children learn from one another as they explore.

Exploring and printing with found objects gives children a chance to observe and describe subtle differences. As the mural paper fills up, children have to look harder for small spaces in which to print. They notice that the little circles can fit inside the big ones, and that the big ones can be printed around the little ones.

Color!

Colored paper, oil pastels, markers, and tempera cakes can be used to add color to prints from any of the chapters. Adding color is a way to encourage children to revisit and expand their work and their ideas.

It is always exciting to bring out an unusual paper or color that children haven't used before. Construction paper and Fadeless™ art paper in assorted colors and sizes 12" x 18" or larger work well.

Oil pastels. Padding cushions the drawing surface, allowing children to easily create more vibrant colors.

Oil pastels add brilliant color to dried prints. They are great for filling in small spaces. Place a newspaper pad under each paper.

Markers can also be used to fill in small spaces on dried prints. Use them to add patterns and decorations to finished work.

Tempera cakes in individual pans are easy to use and exchange. Add water to the pan and keep a brush with each color.

Encourage children to brush over the tempera cake, keeping the bristles in one direction. Size 6 or 7 brushes work well for filling in spaces.

Shannon, age six, printed this name sign. Here you see her adding a border pattern and decorations with colored markers.

A child uses tempera cakes to add color to a group print by four- and five-year-olds.

Painting with Liquid Tempera Paint

Line printing is a great way to develop a structure or composition for painting. Adding paint to printed compositions can create beautiful and dramatic results. Painting is a longer project and requires more work time. When painting, children can get caught up in the excitement, expressiveness, and fluidity of color and paint and can easily lose the line structure that they worked so carefully to create.

✴ I usually suggest that children paint the shapes inside their line compositions. Often, I'll put out oil pastels first for adding color to the smaller shapes before making paint available.

Max created a final print of his houseboat that he painted the following week. As he worked, he exchanged containers of tempera paint with the children at his table. The inviting array of colors was probably one reason that he added the beautiful sunset sky of orange and red to his painting.

A houseboat by Max, age seven. Print (left) and painted print (right).

Willy, age seven, adds paint to his print of the Parthenon.

Gina, age eight, enjoys the option of mixing her colors before adding them to her painting of the Taj Mahal.

▶ video

If you decide to offer liquid tempera paint, first decide how you will distribute the paint, for example, in small jars or in trays.

Jars of tempera paint, each with its own brush, eliminate the need for water. Colors stay purer and children can exchange colors easily. Mix basic colors together to create more unusual colors such as red-orange, lavender, and light blue.

Older children enjoy the option of a tray of paint with many colors so that they can do their own mixing. Ice cube trays work well for this purpose. Remind children to rinse brushes and wipe them on newspaper before going into the next color. This method requires more time for mixing colors and washing and wiping brushes between colors.

A stiff 3/8"-wide easel brush is great for filling in both large and small areas. It is also helpful to have some smaller brushes available for details. Use brushes with short handles to avoid spills.

Direct children on how to paint with the brush (see CD-ROM for demo):

- Stir paint.
- Wipe brush on the inside edge of the container.
- Paint the outline of an area and fill it in, or gently move the brush up and down and from side to side to fill in an area.
- Try to leave the printed lines so that your structure will still be visible.
- Repeat colors to unify the painting and to use up the paint on the brush.
- Replace brush in appropriate jar or rinse, wipe, and start the next color.

Age Level and TWAL Activities

All of the activities in the program are appropriate for pre-K through elementary school children. Part 1 is aimed at younger children, ages four to eight years old, but it can also be used effectively with older elementary school students. The lessons in Part 1 introduce concepts and methods that are extended in each section of Part 2. Part 2 is designed to relate to curriculum areas in the elementary grades. However, pre-K children working on project ideas might find Part 2 appropriate for their research and interests.

When Benjamin (right) was three, he avoided work with studio art materials, preferring to spend time in the block area. Now that he is four and a half, the process of line printing seems to have captured his interest and extended his constructions in block building.

Timing

Each chapter, or lesson, follows the same format and includes an **introduction, motivation, procedure,** and **sequential activities.** For younger children, one or two parts of a lesson at a time will probably be plenty. Additional parts can be added on the days that follow. Older children can move more quickly and can often work through several or all parts of a lesson in a time period of about forty-five minutes. *Breaking down the lesson into parts allows you to pick and choose options as you observe the interest and attention span of your students.*

A general time estimate for each part of the twelve explorations is twenty to forty-five minutes. As children of different ages approach the same project or activity, the time it takes for them to understand the concepts and to practice skills will vary. You will also need to adjust the number and sequencing of steps and the number of materials offered.

As you would do with any new curriculum concept or material, take a few moments to explore line printing yourself before you try it with your students. This will help you feel confident and excited about the process and the possibilities it presents, and will enable you to think through how the setup and flow of a line printing exploration might work in your particular setting.

Room Setup

Cover tables with newspaper. Tape them down in a few places if possible. Place practice paper and a large line printing tool at each place. *Allow a few moments for children to try out the printing process and the strategies for each lesson before handing out trays of paint.* Place trays of ink so that they are within reach of all the children. Give out additional line printing tools or larger sheets of paper when you feel that children are ready, or when papers are very full.

Standing up when printing helps children use the weight of their bodies to print strong, clear lines.

Kindergarten children print with the big line tool. Limiting children to a single printing tool actually opens up unlimited possibilities for construction.

Guidelines for Keeping Hands and Workspaces Clean

Train your students to follow these guidelines for keeping hands and work surfaces orderly. I review the guidelines each time that we print.

1. Rest cardboard against the side of the tray when it is not in use.
2. Put only the inky side of the cardboard into the paint.
3. Pick cardboard up from the clean side when ready to print.

Some teachers keep a stack of damp paper towels handy so that children can wipe their fingers if they get messy.

Teachers with especially large classes can eliminate "passing out paper time" by giving students two or three pieces of paper in a stack. This enables children to move from their practice papers to their next print when they are ready.

Suggestions for Using This Program

Each activity begins with a challenge or a problem to solve. Pay close attention to the sequencing of concepts and materials. The materials that you offer and how and when you make them available matters. Sequencing helps children to focus on one concept at a time. As you pose questions and demonstrate working strategies, listen closely to children's responses. Try to record them. They will help you figure out how your children think and give you ideas about your next area of exploration. Adding a new color, a curved line, or a found object at a key moment renews interest and encourages children to expand ongoing work.

Sequencing the materials that you offer is so important. The children at this table began printing with red paint and the big line tool. Next, the teacher switched colors and printing stamps with another table, giving the children blue paint. Here the teacher offers each child a small found object.

▶ video

Chapter 1, "Basic Lines," stresses teaching/learning strategies and is a good place to begin. Although it focuses on young children, the strategies are universal.

The Teaching/Learning Process

Stepping back to look at and take pleasure in what has been accomplished is an important part of the learning process.

Patrick, age four, is pleased and surprised to see that he has made a window.

The teacher observes his interest. As he finishes, she holds up his paper and says, "Your window really stands out. Can you tell me more about the other lines and shapes you made?"

Patrick begins to describe other structures that he notices when he steps away from his work. "This window is in my garage."

Following these suggestions will enhance the teaching/learning process:

- Observe, listen, and record children's words and constructions as they make discoveries and insights.
- Revisit the activity through discussion of children's work.
- Pose questions about the basic lines and the thinking process behind children's constructions.
- Use a descriptive, rather than evaluative, vocabulary in your interactions with children.
- Save a memory of key experiences to share with children and parents. The three photos shown on page 13 exemplify all the children's excitement in constructing and building with shapes.

Part 1

Thinking with a Line

David, at age five, discovers that he can construct all kinds of structures with the line printing process.

This section of the program demonstrates strategies for working with materials while introducing the process of line printing to children.

Program Objectives
The engaging activities in *Thinking with a Line* are designed to encourage and lead children to:

● **Explore**   spatial relationships
the beginnings of literacy
geometrical thinking
the mathematics of design

● **Construct**   shapes and buildings
letters, names, and words
the alphabet
patterns and radial designs

● **Develop**   understanding of line as a basic element of
design and construction
creative and critical thinking skills
experience with materials

15

David, at age three, explores line printing for the first time at a table set up for group work.

Chapter 1
Basic Lines

Training the Hands, Eyes, and Mind

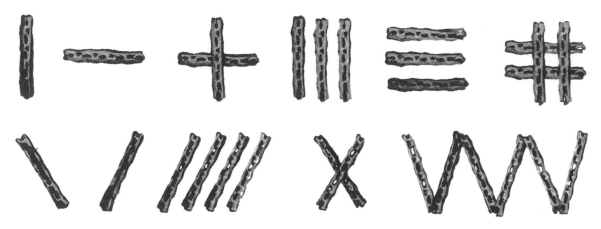

Begin with the basic lines. Printing the basic lines lays the groundwork for all of the activities. Practicing these lines again and again in multiple ways, and inventing one's own lines, trains hands, minds, and eyes to work together.

Supplies

- large line tool to begin
- small straight line tool to add later
- 9" x 12" practice paper
- 12" x 18" second sheet
- 1 color of paint (a second color in reserve)
- Styrofoam trays
- chart of the basic lines, as shown above

Learning Objectives
Printing the basic lines introduces children to:

- the importance of hand orientation, placement, and spacing
- the process of making a clear print
- the idea of repetition
- a line vocabulary
- an awareness of different kinds of lines

 On the CD-ROM

Under BASIC LINES

Vertical/Horizontal
Diagonal
Smooshing
Watch a Teacher
    Introduction
    Provoking Thinking
    Making a Connection
Teaching and Learning
    Observe, Listen, Record
    Revisiting Line Printing
    Follow-up Questions
    Notes on Language
Common Lines
Next Steps
Related Projects
    Line Games
    Line Collage
    Music

Activity 1

Introducing and Practicing Vertical and Horizontal Lines

Up and down . . . sideways

Motivation   Point out to children that lines are all around us. Have children look around the room—at the walls, floors, and at one another's clothing. Can they find any lines? (Use the basic lines as a reference.)

Procedure   Introduce and demonstrate horizontal and vertical lines, and allow time for the children to practice them. (Use the four-step process illustrated on page 3 —Dip into paint. Press firmly onto paper. Lift. Repeat.) Start on practice paper.

Watch a teacher engage children as she introduces this new tool and process for children to explore.

▶ video

Children intuitively understand the importance of hand orientation as they begin to experiment with line printing. Clearly demonstrate the difference between vertical and horizontal lines with your hand and a line tool and encourage children to try the following kinds of lines and to discover others.

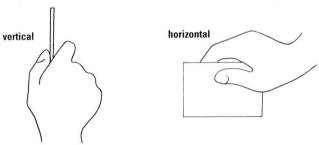

vertical   horizontal

|||| **A row of vertical lines**

☰ ☰   **Stacks of horizontal lines**

⌗ ┼   **Crossing lines**

— — — —   **A broken line**

————————   **A long line**

✱ Demonstrate only what is necessary to introduce the process and the concepts that children need to get started. An open-ended demonstration provokes enthusiasm and ideas, allowing children to make their own discoveries. When you see children running out of space, hand out the small line tool or another piece of paper.

Activity 2

Introducing and Practicing Diagonal Lines

Motivation

Call attention to, discuss, and demonstrate diagonal lines when you notice them appearing in children's work.

Procedure

Demonstrate and invite children to practice printing.

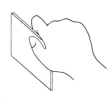

✱ Diagonal lines are trickier than horizontal and vertical lines for young learners to print and use in their constructions. Practice printing diagonal lines without ink first so that children have the idea before they begin. Using the diagrams shown at right, model how to print a row of diagonal lines. Tell children to try printing lines that slant to the left, then to the right. Demonstrate crossing lines, a zigzag, and a long diagonal line.

 A row of diagonal lines

 Try one way and then the other

 Try crossing lines

 Try a zig zag

 Try a long diagonal line

A small group of four- and five-year-olds practiced printing horizontal, vertical, and diagonal lines on a large piece of paper.

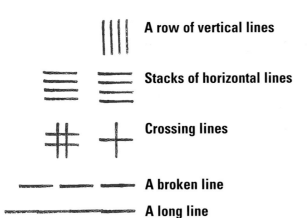

Activity 3

Adding Complexity

Offer the smaller straight line printing tool or a second color, and encourage children to add to their explorations. The small line tool is handy for connecting lines and for trying out smaller versions of the basic lines. No doubt children will discover other ways to use this new tool. Make sure that smaller lines are half the size of the longer line.

If possible, record descriptions and titles.

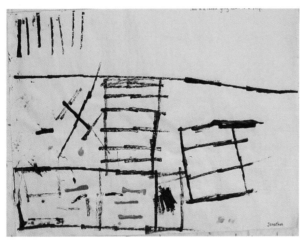

"This is a ladder going down to a ship," says Jonathan, age six.

"The stars are snowflakes and the triangles are mountains covered with snow," says Emma, age six.

✱ As children begin exploring, you might see them dragging and twisting the cardboard or painting with it. This is developmentally appropriate, and it is exciting. Children often discover interesting effects that they can work into their prints later on. However, these actions are not printing actions. In order to explore the potential of line printing, refocus children's attention on developing printing skills. Or, spend some time painting with the cardboard, and choose another day to begin line printing.

Follow-up 1

Revisit Children's Work

Allow time for children to revisit and share their work with one another. Hold up line prints and invite children to explain their thought processes. Ask, "Can you show us where you began and how you developed your idea."

Revisiting provides opportunities to

• reinforce basic line concepts
• use and build a descriptive vocabulary
• understand what children have discovered and learned
• generate ideas for further exploration
• appreciate the multiple ways that children use the same materials

Sequoia, age seven, discusses the wildlife sanctuary that he portrayed in his print.

Stepping back from ongoing work lets children see what they have been doing from a new perspective. Sharing work and ideas allows children to stop and think about what they have accomplished and to consider what they plan to do next. Sharing allows you to learn more about children's interests, ways of working, and thinking. This generates excitement among peers, and project ideas are likely to emerge. Sharing work from a previous exploration is a sure way to provoke new interest and energy and reinforce skills and strategies.

As children share their experiences, ask them questions that help them think about their working process, rather than questions that can be answered with a simple yes or no.

The teacher asks, "Avery, would you point out the first line that you printed? I'm curious about where you began printing."

Questions about mechanics
Can you show us how to make a clear, clean print? Show us the best place to hold your cardboard when printing.
• How much ink is enough? too much? too little?
• How hard do you need to press?
• Why did you stand up to print?

Questions about the basic lines
Show us with your hand how you would print
• a row of vertical lines
• a stack of horizontal lines
• a diagonal line
• a zigzag line
• a long line

Questions about the thinking process
Did anyone try connecting? What happened?
What are some discoveries you made while you were experimenting?

Show us how you printed that shape or design. What gave you the idea? What would you like to try printing next time?

Follow-up 2

As children explore line, and articulate their discoveries, they become more aware of line in their environment. Bringing works of art, based on similar concepts into the classroom can spark new associations, rich discussions, and additional questions and ideas. When children's work ideas are appreciated, celebrated, and respected, they in turn respect and appreciate the achievements of other artists.

Books

Hoban, Tana. *Spirals, Curves, Fanshapes & Lines*. New York: Greenwillow Books, 1992.

Johnson, Crockett. *A Picture for Harold's Room*. New York: Scholastic, 1973.

Juster, Norton. *The Dot and the Line*. New York: Random House, 1963.

MacAgy, Elizabeth. *Going for a Walk with a Line: A Step into the World of Modern Art*. New York: Doubleday & Company, 1959.

Russo, Marisabina. *The Line Up Book*. New York: Greenwillow Books, 1986.

Schaefer, Carole Lexa, and Pierre Morgan, *The Squiggle*. New York: Crown Publishers, 1996.

Yenawine, Philip. *Lines*. New York: The Museum of Modern Art, 1991.

Chapter 2
Constructing Shapes

When lines touch, a shape is born.

Learning to make shapes opens up the world of geometry and construction. Children develop their own strategies and gain respect for the ideas of their classmates when they work together to explore multiple solutions to the problem of how to use a line stamp to create a shape.

Supplies

- large line tool to begin
- small line tool to add later
- 9" x 12" practice paper
- 12" x 18" or 18" x 24" second sheet of paper
- trays
- 1 color of paint to start. Have another color of paint handy if you want to introduce a second color. Or, give half of the children one color of paint and half another color. Switch the paint trays and cardboard tools halfway through exploration.

Learning Objectives
When constructing shapes, children develop and practice

- hand orientation
- placement skills
- understanding of spacing
- planning
- understanding the differences among shapes
- multiple ways to solve a problem
- names of geometric shapes
- using a beginning math vocabulary
- seeing the relationship between shapes

 On the CD-ROM

Under SHAPES

Discovering Shapes
Squares
Triangles
Watch a Teacher
Next Steps
    Repeating Shapes
    A Connecting Exercise
    Transferring Strategies
Related Projects
    A Shape Game
    Tape a Shape
    Paper Strips

Activity 1

Squares: Two Strategies

Motivation Initiate a shape-making adventure by asking, "How could you use the process of line printing to make a square?" Listen for multiple solutions. Demonstrate as children suggest ideas.

Procedure Demonstrate and invite children to practice printing squares. Two different solutions are shown in this activity.

Strategy One

Children who haven't yet drawn a square often discover squares using this strategy.

Begin by printing two vertical, parallel lines.

Connect them with horizontal lines.

Strategy Two

To demonstrate or use this strategy, children have to understand the properties of a square.

 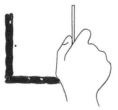

Start with a right angle made with one vertical and one horizontal line that touch.

Connect with a second vertical line and a second horizontal line.

Have children practice by repeating the shapes.

Encourage children to build upon their explorations by asking, "Can you print a bigger square? a smaller square? Can you print inside a big square or around a small square? How could you make a rectangle?"

Activity 2

Triangles

Motivation   Invite children to describe or demonstrate multiple solutions to the problem of how to construct a triangle, or three-sided shape.

Zoeth (above), age six, prints a triangular roof for a building.

Vivi (right), age six, builds out from an equilateral triangle.

Children often use surprising language to describe their creations. I overheard Ezekiel, age six, saying, "I'm working on shapes that don't exist."

Procedure   Let the children describe their own directions for creating a triangle. Follow their directions to demonstrate multiple strategies.

Listen for children's unique names for different kinds of triangles and record them. With older children you may wish to identify and define particular kinds of triangles such as equilateral (a triangle with three equal sides) or isosceles (a triangle with two equal sides).

Because the sides of a triangle are diagonal lines, triangles are more difficult to construct than squares or rectangles. As children experiment, they are likely to print other shapes. Celebrate shape discoveries and share them with the rest of the class in the same way that you might celebrate work with manipulative materials such as pattern blocks.

Activity 3

A Connecting Exercise

Motivation
This exercise helps children experiment with shapes and space. It generates unusual shapes while encouraging children to continue exploring.

Procedure
Demonstrate these directions as you discuss them:

1. Start at the edge of your paper.
2. Print a line.
3. Each line that you add must
   • connect to the last line, or
   • connect to another line, or
   • touch an edge of the paper.

When they have finished, encourage them to look between the lines. Ask, "What shapes can you make?"

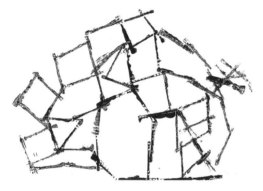

When she stepped back to look at her work, Naomi said, "The squares are windows!"

✱ Older children can identify, name, and define other geometric shapes such as pentagons, hexagons, and octagons as they appear. Ask, "How do you know that this shape is a _____? What are its identifying properties or attributes?"

Follow-up

Place prints on tables or easels and invite children to paint the shapes that they like best.

Emma, age four, paints in the shapes that she finds in a group print from the preceding day.

Books

Burns, Marilyn, and Gordon Silveria. *The Greedy Triangle*. New York: Scholastic, 1994.

Falwell, Cathryn. *Shape Space*. New York: Clarion Books, 1992. (Note: A young dancer dances her way among geometric shapes.)

Greene, Rhonda Gowler. *When a Line Bends . . . A Shape Begins*. Boston: Houghton Mifflin Co., 1997.

———. *Circles, Triangles and Squares*. New York: Macmillan Publishing Co., 1974.

Hoban, Tana. *So Many Circles, So Many Squares*. New York: Greenwillow Books, 1998.

Karlin, Bernie. *Shapes*. New York: Simon and Schuster, 1992.

Lerner, Sharon. *Square Is a Shape*. Minneapolis, MN: Lerner Publications Company, 1974.

Onyefulu, Ifeonma. *A Triangle for Adaora: An African Book of Shapes*. Dutton, 2000. (Note: A Nigerian girl named Ugo teaches her cousin Adaora about shapes using objects around their village. Includes explanatory notes.)

Smith, Mavis. *Crescents*. New York: Warner Books, Inc., 1991.

Smoothey, Marion. *Let's Investigate Shapes*. New York: Marshall Cavendish, 1993.

Steele, Margaret, and Cindy Estes. *The Art of Shapes*. Los Angeles: The Museum of Contemporary Art, 1997.

Tompert, Ann. Illustrated by Robert Andrew Parker. *Grandfather Tang's Story*. New York: Crow Publishers, Inc., 1990.

Yenawine, Philip. *Shapes*. New York: Museum of Modern Art/Delacorte, 1991.

Chapter 3
Constructing Letters

MNTV

"They're all lines!"

Ben, age four and a
half, discovers the
letter H.

While exploring line printing, four-year-old Isabel began constructing letters. As a result of this experience she made an important discovery—"They're all lines!" She's absolutely right. The letters of the alphabet are simply vertical, horizontal, diagonal, and curved lines connected and arranged in agreed-upon configurations. In order to print each letter, children use analytical thinking skills to figure out the direction, position, and spacing of each line. Line printing is a concrete way for children to see, physically feel, and demonstrate these complex understandings on paper.

Supplies

- large line tool to begin
- large curved line tool
- small line and small curve tool to add later
- 9" x 12" practice paper
- 12" x 18" or longer second sheet of paper for printing names
- 1 color of paint
- trays

Learning Objectives

When printing letters, children develop and practice

- hand orientation
- proper hand grip and pressure
- placement skills
- spatial awareness
- printing curved lines
- analytical thinking skills
- planning
- letter recognition
- letter construction
- understanding of the differences among letters

 On the CD-ROM

Under LETTERS

Straight-edge
Letter Designs
Adding a Curve
Names
    Planning
    Practicing
    Children's Strategies
The Alphabet
Upper- & Lowercase Letters
    Children's Strategies
Next Steps
    Colored Paper
    Name Signs
    Decorating Names

Activity 1

Straight-Edge Letters

Motivation

While printing basic lines, a few children are sure to print a letter. Use these children's inventions as springboards to initiate an exploration of printed letters. The first time that you explore letters with line printing, begin simply with the big line tool. Let the discoveries come from the children.

If possible, begin with the letters that are easy to construct, such as those that are made with vertical and horizontal lines.

Procedure

Discuss and invite children to share strategies for constructing letters. It helps to personalize the experience by choosing a straight-edged letter from each child's name, and asking, "Do you think you could figure out how to print a _____?"

The diagonal lines make the following letters trickier to construct.

AKMNVWXYZ

Activity 2

Finding Letters

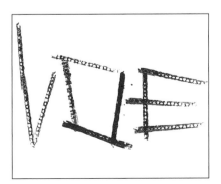

Hold up children's letter explorations and invite them to play a game of finding and pointing out the hidden letters in each other's prints. Often young children don't realize that they have printed a letter until someone points it out to them.

Sometimes children figure out how to use the big line tool to print letters whose shapes include curves (C, D, O), as Joe, age four, did in this example. Be sure to give reinforcement to this inventive way of thinking.

Activity 3

Constructing Letters with Curved Lines

BCDGJOPQRSU

Motivation   Introduce the curved line tool and discuss the possibilities offered by a curved line.

When I held up the large line tool, I was amazed to hear a chorus of children saying, "Now I can make my P (or D, S, J, C, and so on)." The children intuitively understood that they needed a curve. Adding a curve opens many new options for letter construction.

Procedure   Identify letters with curves and discuss construction strategies. Ask children which letters they think will be the most difficult to print. Discuss strategies for making those letters (B, D, G, J, P Q, R, S) and demonstrate by following children's suggestions. Children appreciate knowing that they are tackling difficult problems and that you have confidence in their ability to solve those problems.

Allow time for children to practice experimenting with this new tool. Children will discover letters as they explore.

▶ video   The best time to add a curve is when you observe that children need it.

▶ video   Curved lines are more difficult to manipulate and place than straight lines.

Activity 4

Making a Letter Chart

Invite children to make a chart of letters with at least one curve as a reference for the classroom.

Manipulating a curve is a concrete way to tackle the problem of letter reversal. By changing hand position, children get a feel for direction and can see and feel the effects of their actions. Be sure to try this yourself before trying it with children.

Activity 5

Letter Designs

Motivation   Initiate a letter design exploration with a whole class, or suggest this to individual children when you observe that they are ready for a new challenge. You might discover letter designs within the children's explorations that you can use to jumpstart this exploration. In fact, this lesson came about because a kindergarten teacher noticed that her students were enjoying repeating a letter many times and making designs out of the letters. They were actually playing with the letters. She encouraged them to build upon this idea.

Procedure   Suggest that students begin with a favorite letter and build a design around it. Turning the paper around as they work can help the design process.

Angela, age five, printed a design using the letters A, E, and C.

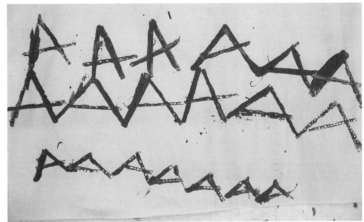

This kindergarten child printed a pattern of big and little A's.

Follow-up 1

To extend work with letters, ask children to try printing the letters in their names.

Follow-up 2

When you notice that children have an interest in forming different letters, you might set up a situation that allows them to try printing the entire alphabet.

Teachers interviewed the children who elected to try this activity. Here are excerpts from an interview with Nolan.

Nolan, age five and a half, said, "The printing went fine. I might have had to do a little cheating. (We asked the children to try to print—as opposed to draw—all the parts of the letters.) I had to use the edge for making the G. The trickiest part was making the P 'cause I had to get the smallest turn (curved line)."

"Did you need the alphabet to help you remember how to make some of the letters?"

"No. I already had the alphabet in my head."

✱ Notice that the teacher placed each line and curve tool into a separate tray of ink so that they would be easy for children to locate, use, and replace.

Books

Johnson, Stephen T. *Alphabet City.* New York: Viking, 1995.
Lobel, Arnold. *On Market Street.* New York: Greenwillow, 1981.
MacDonald, Susie. *Alphabatics.* New York: Aladdin Books, 1992.
Pelletier, David. *The Graphic Alphabet.* New York: Orchard, 1996.
Rankin, Laura. *The Handmade Alphabet.* New York: Dial Books, 1991.
Tryon, Leslie. *Albert Builds an Alphabet.* New York: Simon & Schuster, 1991.

Chapter 4

Pattern and Design

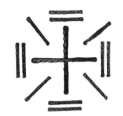

A design is the arrangement of forms according to a plan. To design is to play with the intersection of one's own ideas and a set of rules.

Jeremy, age five, enjoys sorting and arranging a pile of smooth round stones.

Young children are designers by nature. If you watch children working on their own at a drawing/writing center, you will notice that they often invest time and derive satisfaction from creating elaborate designs. They also spend time and attention sorting, ordering, and arranging collections of stones, shells, sticks, and small toys. These are early mathematical and aesthetic explorations. They fulfill the natural urge to create order and beauty.

Children also enjoy learning about and experimenting with formal ways of creating patterns, radial designs, and other design formations.

Supplies

- large line tool to begin
- small line tool to add later
- 6" x 18" practice paper for printing patterns
- 12" x 12" practice paper for printing radials
- 12" x 18" or larger paper for printing patterns
- 18" x 18" squares for printing radial designs
- 1 color of paint to start, a second color of paint to add if you need it
- trays
- found objects, one per child

Learning Objectives
When creating patterns and radial designs, children develop and practice
- hand orientation, placement, and spatial skills
- planning
- working with a set of rules
- using mathematical variables such as number, grouping, direction, alternation, position, and length
- analytical thinking skills
- systematic approaches to building from a core design

💿 On the CD-ROM
Under DESIGNS

Child Designers
Patterns
  Printing Patterns
  Watch a Teacher
  Add Color
  Found Object
  Switch Colors
  Next Steps
Radial Designs
  Printing Radials
  Examples
  Drawing Radials

Children's Strategies
  Length
  Stars
  Alternating
  Circles
  Taking Time to Think
  Combination
  Extending
Related Projects
  Wrapping Paper
  Frames

Pattern

Motivation Define the concept of pattern by posing the question "What is a pattern?" (A pattern is formed when an element is repeated many times in the same way.)

Procedure Bring something with distinct patterns into the classroom. Ask the children to identify the patterns and to analyze why the lines, shapes, and colors make up a pattern. Ask, "Where do you see a pattern? What repeats?"

This cloth was woven on a back-strap loom by Margarita Lopez y Lopez from San Antonio Aguas Calientes, Guatemala.

This cloth contains a central, informal design of flowers, vertical bars of patterned zigzags and diamonds, and stripe patterns on the horizontal borders. When seen as a whole, the entire cloth is a symmetrical design. Children have a great time searching for patterns and making distinctions between different kinds of designs. It is the challenge of looking closely and using language to support a position that is important. It doesn't matter so much if they are actually right or wrong. They will look more closely at pattern and design in the world around them after an activity such as this.

Patterns are everywhere, especially in textiles, clothing, pottery, and jewelry from all over the world. To explore pattern is to have a window into the world's rich cultural heritage.

A few children will probably print a pattern during line printing explorations. You can also use those children's work to launch a pattern printing exploration.

Look around your home for examples. You are sure to find patterns on clothing, furniture, textiles, and pottery.

Activity 1

Printing Patterns

Motivation   Line printing is an easy way to practice making patterns and to gain a concrete understanding of how to create and change a pattern.

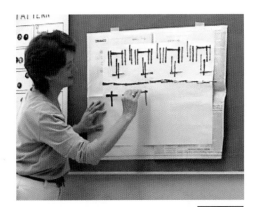

▶ video

Procedure   Demonstrate the following directions as you discuss them.

Watch a video clip of a teacher discussing and demonstrating pattern directions with a group of first-grade children.

Repeat a line, with equal space between lines, all the way across your paper.

Change the number in a grouping.

Change the position. Go up or down.

Change the direction. Use vertical, horizontal, and diagonal lines.

Alternate lines and spaces.

Use a horizontal line to divide patterns.

To extend work with patterning, add one or more of the following: the small line tool, a second color, or a small found object, one per child.

Activity 2
Radial Designs

Motivation

Begin by discussing and defining the properties of a radial design and the differences between a pattern and a radial design.

Radial designs start at a center point and radiate out like the rays of the sun or the spokes of a wheel. Radial designs build upon patterning concepts and skills. However, they are more complex and more difficult to create than patterns since the position and spatial orientation of the lines are always changing.

Procedure

Provide paper that is 12" x 12" or larger. Demonstrate the following directions and allow time for students to practice.

- Start with **+** or **X** in the middle of your paper.
- Repeat the same line in the same position in each wedge. Turning the paper as you work helps with placement.
- Try changing the direction, number, position, and spacing of lines as you work.
- Try crossing and connecting.
- Work out to the edge of the paper.

You will notice that despite good intentions, most of the children's designs will not be perfectly regular—and that is okay! What is important is to work with the concepts and to have the experience. As children continue to create radial designs—and I have found that children of all ages love to do this—their designs will grow more exact and complex. Be sure to enjoy and celebrate the unique designs that children do evolve. As children point out the unique features of their patterns or radial designs, you will be amazed by their ingenious descriptions. You might also spot symmetrical designs and beautiful asymmetrical compositions.

Everyone enjoys creating radial designs because the results are so appealing.

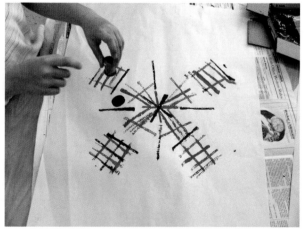

To extend work with radial design, add one or more of the following: the small line tool, another color, or a found object.

Follow-up

After practicing patterns or radial designs, try printing on colored paper using one or more new paint colors to add interest and excitement. Expanding the number of colors works when children have already practiced designing. They become aware of and interested in the beauty and complexity they are able to create using a set of mathematical guidelines.

The teacher offered 18" x 24" blue construction paper and different-colored paints after the children had spent several days practicing ways to create patterns.

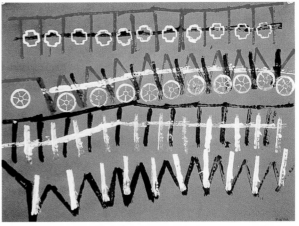

Each table began with one color and the large line tool. During the exploration, printing colors were switched, along with the line tools and found objects.

Books

Chocolate, Deborah M. Newton, and John Ward. *Kente Colors*. New York: Walker and Company, 1996. (Note: A rhyming description of the kente cloth costumes of the Ashanti and Ewe people of Ghana and a portrayal of the symbolic colors and patterns.)

Esbensen, Barbara Juster, and Helen Davie. *Echoes for the Eye: Poems to Celebrate Patterns in Nature*. New York: HarperCollins, 1996.

Murphy, Stuart, and Lois Ehlert. *A Pair of Socks*. New York: HarperCollins, 1996.

Palmer, Dennis. *Introducing Pattern, Its Development and Application*. New York: Watson-Guptill, 1970.

Smoothey, Marion. *Let's Investigate Shape Patterns*. New York: Marshall Cavendish, 1993.

Yates, Irene. *All About Pattern*. New York: Benchmark Books, 1997.

Chapter 5
Building with Shapes

Houses and buildings are common themes in children's representational work.

As children print shapes, connect them, and add to them, buildings and other structures begin to emerge. Once children have developed the skill of printing shapes, they are ready to intentionally construct a building or structure.

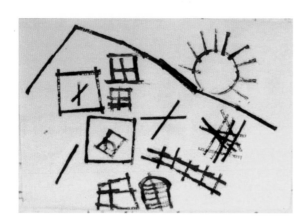

"It's my attic and those are boxes of stuff,"
says Henry, age five.

Supplies

- large line tool to begin
- small straight line tool to add later
- 12" x 18" practice paper
- 12" x 18" colored paper
- 1 color of paint
- tray

Learning Objectives
When building with shapes, children develop and practice

- hand orientation and spatial awareness
- placement and printing skills
- constructing a variety of geometric shapes
- an awareness of shapes in the environment
- recognizing and recreating structures in the built environment
- integrating a variety of line, shape, and design elements

 On the CD-ROM

Under BUILDINGS

Getting Started
Time to Practice
Children's Strategies
  Foundation
  Connecting Shapes
  Filling
  Contour
  Main Large Shapes
  Details
  Alternative Ideas
Next Steps
  Big Paper
  Small Lines
  Found Object
  Add Paint
  Cut Shapes
Related Projects
  Drawing Blocks
  Cityscapes 1
  Cityscapes 2
  Observational Drawing

Analyze a Building

Motivation

Looking closely at a building by picking out the main shapes is an exercise in analytical thinking.

Procedure

Guide students to look at a building and identify the geometric shapes. Ask questions to help children focus.

What are the largest shapes?
What shapes are the windows?
How are the rectangles different from one another?

Recall strategies and directions for constructing squares, triangles, rectangles, and other shapes with line printing tools.

Blocks can serve as a helpful reference.

Find a nearby building or a picture of a building in which the shapes are very clear and easy to see. Study the building for a minute, and then ask, "What shapes and lines do you notice?"

Activity 1

Practice Building with Shapes

Motivation   Invite children to share their ideas about how to begin creating a building using the line stamp as a construction tool. Demonstrate strategies as children suggest them.

Procedure   Encourage children to practice constructing. The illustrations show sample strategies.

Begin with an outline.

Begin with the foundation.

Build up with shapes.

Try different shapes and sizes.

Offer a smaller line tool when you observe that children need it to add details to their structures.

Activity 2

Interviews: Honoring Children's Ideas and Work

Interviewing helps children to revisit and reflect on an experience. Talking to children seriously about their work helps teachers and parents understand and appreciate each child in a deeper way. Interviews reveal a variety of solutions to the problem of how to construct a building. Use questioning strategies such as, "Tell me about your line print. How did you do it? Where did you begin?" Posting quotes from interviews and displaying them with the child's work is a powerful way to document the learning process and students' reflective thinking.

Lena constructs a building.

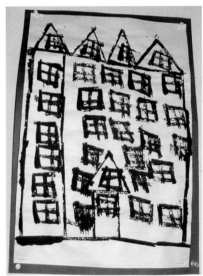

Hotel by Lena, age five.

"I was making a hotel that people live in if they don't have a home. First I started at the bottom, then I went straight on the side. The black thing that's really black (dark blotch on the bottom) is where the smoke came out. It's like a chimney. I made lots of windows because lots of people lived there."

Asking student teachers, aides, or parents to interview children and record their thoughts is a great way for them to help out in the classroom. This provides an important service to teachers, and at the same time offers an opportunity to learn more about the intelligence and creative ideas of young children.

Newly printed structures can stimulate older children to write a paragraph or even a story about their buildings.

Activity 3

Print Again on a New Color

Motivation   Printing on a new color of paper can often motivate children to continue working.

Procedure   When children have finished practicing, display a variety of colored papers at least 12" x 18" and invite them to choose a color of paper on which to print.

Anthony, age five, practices building with shapes on newsprint.

His building grows more complex with the addition of each shape.

Choosing a new color paper encourages Anthony to continue constructing.

Activity 4

Adding Color Details with Oil Pastels

Motivation   Once prints have dried, children enjoy revisiting their work by adding color with drawing tools. Oil pastels work well to add color to small places.

Some children will spend a great deal of time coloring, whereas others are happy with a few bright spots of color. You will notice that color can add an emotional dimension to children's work.

Procedure   Pad work surfaces with newspaper to make coloring with oil pastels easier.

Even one or two small areas of color can add interest to a print. Since small hands can tire quickly, encourage children to select a few shapes or special places that they want to highlight with color.

✱ There are many subtle ways to encourage a child to continue an investigation. Simply changing the orientation of the paper from horizontal to vertical can open up a different way of looking at and thinking about space.

Here is Anthony's completed building. Notice how many shapes he colored and how carefully he worked.

Follow-up

Add Buildings to a Mural

After children have experimented with the idea of constructing a building using the process of line printing, they enjoy adding buildings and other constructions to a group mural. If you decide to try this, suggest that children start at the bottom of the paper and build up with shapes.

Parents create buildings during a parent workshop.

Here is a section of the mural created by the parents. Notice that some buildings were cut out and added later. Parents also discovered ways to add trees and people.

The parents shown on page 43 experienced the learning process by painting their own buildings on mural paper. Doing an activity with parents helps them understand the thinking and learning that go into their children's studio artwork. It also promotes support and advocacy for education and the arts.

Books

Barton, Byron. *Building A House.* New York: Greenwillow Books, 1981.
Florian, Douglas. *The City.* New York: Cromwell Junior Books, 1982.
Johnson, Stephen. *City by Numbers.* New York: Viking, 1998.
Potts, Jim. *The House That Makes Shapes.* Tucson: Harbinger House, 1992.

Part 2

Creating with a Line

Jonah, age eight, tells me that he is making the Eiffel Tower.

This section of the program demonstrates strategies for using the process of line printing to perceive and create structures in the built and natural environments.

Program Objectives
Projects encourage and lead children to:

● **Explore**   composition
advertising
snow crystals
anatomy
branching patterns in nature
symmetry
architecture

● **Construct**   signs and posters
six-sided snowflakes
skeletons
trees
columns, pediments, arches,
    domes
vehicles and machines

● **Develop**   facility with line printing
imaginative ways to use the line
    printing tools
creative and critical thinking skills
visual literacy
a descriptive vocabulary

Children are ready to apply line printing skills to more complex problems when they feel confident with the process. Review printing techniques and guidelines for keeping workspaces orderly each time that you introduce one of these lessons.

Chapter 6
Composition

Patricia A. Renick, *Garden Dancers,* 1995. Welded steel painted black.

In most works of art the composition—arrangement of the art elements line, shape, color, texture, and value—is informal or asymmetrical. We don't see a pattern or radial design. However, the composition seems to be balanced and pleasing. Artists balance their compositions by instinctively adjusting the placement of each art element as it is added.

Supplies

- large and small line tools
- large and small curves
- 9" x 12" practice paper
- 12" x 18" second sheet of paper
- 1 color of paint to start, a second color of paint to add if you need it
- trays
- found objects in reserve

Learning Objectives
When students experiment with the art elements line and shape and with principles of composition, they develop

- an intuitive sense of design, balance, placement, and spacing
- the ability to use elements and principles of art in a composition
- a descriptive visual arts vocabulary
- analytical thinking skills
- facility with line printing tools

 On the CD-ROM

Under COMPOSITION

Analyzing
Practicing
Printing
    Observe
    Related Projects
    Designing with a Collection of
      Objects

47

Analyze a Composition

Motivation   A guided discussion of a nonobjective work of art can help children understand the kinds of judgments artists make as they create a composition.
Studying a nonobjective composition necessitates the use of a visual arts
vocabulary. In order to describe the differences and similarities among lines,
shapes, textures, colors, and values, children and teachers alike must use
descriptive adjectives and adverbs to describe the positions, directions, subtleties, and effects of the art elements that they see.

Wassily Kandinsky,
Untitled (Drawing for
"Diagram 17"), 1925.
Black ink on ivory
paper. Courtesy of the
Mount Holyoke College
Art Museum, South
Hadley, MA. © 2005
Artists Rights Society
(ARS) New York/ADAGP,
Paris.

Procedure   Initiate a discussion by asking questions such as the following:

- Can you point out and describe the different kinds of lines that you see in
  this drawing?
- What lines and shapes repeat? What effect does this have? (Repetitions are
  pleasing and tend to unify a composition.)
- Can you describe the ways in which the repeated lines and shapes differ
  from each other? (Length, direction, thickness, solid, open.)
- Why do you think the artist made them different? (Differences create contrast and variety, making compositions more interesting to look at.)
- Are there any lines or shapes that do not repeat?

✱ The artist who created this carefully balanced composition is credited with
inventing a revolutionary new form of art known as nonobjective art.
Nonobjective art is an arrangement of pure lines and shapes that have no rec-
ognizable subject matter. Kandinsky believed that lines, shapes, and other elements of art could be used as symbols to communicate.

Activity 1

Practice Composing

Motivation

Discuss ways in which the organizing principles—rhythm or repetition, balance, variety, contrast, emphasis, and direction or motion—are concepts that help artists think about how to arrange lines and shapes in a composition.

Using only lines to compose narrows the focus at the same time as it expands the possibilities. Name some of the lines and shapes that children discovered in their earlier explorations with the process of line printing.

Procedure

Practice using the line printing tools to break up and design the space on your paper. Depending on the age and experience of your students, decide how many line tools to offer and when to offer them for this experience.

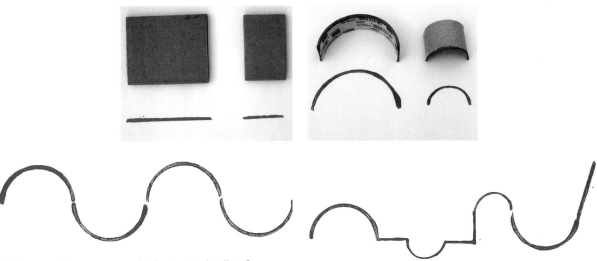

What unusual lines can you print by connecting lines?

What unusual shapes can you create with the line tools?

Revisit the explorations in line printing with the children. Notice interesting lines, shapes, and ways of using the tools. Ask children to demonstrate their strategy for creating a particularly unusual line, shape, or effect.

Jake, age six, explores the possibilities of a curve.

Rowen, age five, explores a different way of using the curved line tool.

Activity 2

Print a Composition

Motivation   Demonstrate how to work practice prints into a composition, or begin again on a larger piece of paper. Think about the organizing principles of repetition, balance, variety, contrast, emphasis, and direction or motion as children work.

Procedure   Encourage children to repeat lines and shapes to unify and balance their designs. Suggest that they change the length, size, direction, spacing, and number of times they repeat a line or shape to add variety and interest to their compositions.

Exploration with curves by Rowen, age five.

Rabbit by Naomi, age nine.

You will probably notice that children have created both nonobjective (nonrepresentational) and realistic compositions. Invite children to tell what gave them the idea for their composition, and where they began.

Activity 3

Add Color

Motivation   You may wish to hand out containers of tempera paint and invite children to fill in the spaces between their lines. This step often works best if prints have had time to dry first.

Procedure   When preparing children to paint, encourage them to

- keep the beauty of their lines visible
- fill in the areas between the lines with color
- repeat each color in several places to unify the composition
- add interest by varying the size and number of areas that they paint with a color

Follow-up

Aritst Paul Klee uses line to create volume and texture in this whimsical drawing.

Paul Klee, *Goat,* 1925, 8⅝" x 11¹⁄₁₆". Brush and watercolor, some applied with atomizer, on smooth coated paper laid down on beige wove paper sheet. Smith College Museum of Art, Northampton, Massachusetts.

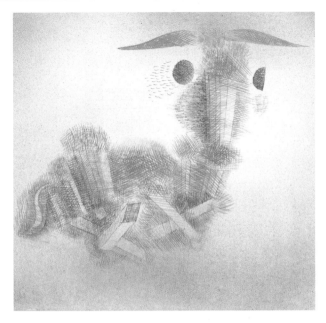

Observe and discuss works of art by artists who create nonobjective or abstract works of art, such as Paul Klee, Piet Mondrian, Wassily Kandinsky, and Sol Lewitt. Notice the kinds of lines used and how they are varied. Notice other art elements—shape, color, texture, and value—and where they appear in the work of art.

✱ Ask children to point out art elements that repeat, areas that stand out, and movements or motions. Ask, "Why do you think the artist used the art element in that particular way?" "What makes the composition pleasing to look at?"

Books

Freeman, Don. *Norman the Doorman.* New York: Viking Press, 1959.

Johnson, Crockett. *A Picture for Harold's Room.* New York: Scholastic, 1960.

Lehn, Barbara. *What Is an Artist?* Brookfield, CT: Millbrook Press, 2002.

Raczka, Bob. *No One Saw—Ordinary Things through the Eyes of an Artist.* Brookfield, CT: Millbrook Press, 2002.

Venezia, Mike. *Henri Matisse.* Chicago: Children's Press, 1991.

———. *Paul Klee.* Chicago: Children's Press, 1991.

Wehrli, Ursus. *Kunst Aufraumen.* (English Version, *Tidying Up Art*) London: Prestel, 2003. (Note: Wehrli "decomposes" works of art into shapes, colors, etc.)

Chapter 7
Signs and Posters

This sign was created during a parent workshop.

Children often have a need to create posters to advertise classroom, school, or community events. Line printing is an easy and effective way to create bold and clear signs and posters. It is also a great way to practice the many skills and concepts involved in letter formation and writing.

Supplies

- large and small line tools
- large and small curves
- 9" x 12" or larger practice paper
- 12" x 18" or larger paper
- 1 color of paint to start, a second color of paint to add if you need it
- trays

On the CD-ROM

Under SIGNS AND POSTERS

Planning
Printing

Learning Objectives
When designing and creating signs or posters, children practice and explore

- principles of advertising
- awareness of signs and posters as a means of communication and persuasion
- ways to communicate a message with few words
- symbols
- proper spelling
- spacing and layout
- planning

Analyze a Sign or Poster

Motivation

Look at a few select signs or posters and pose some questions to initiate a discussion. Or collect shopping bags with common logos. Even young students recognize brand names. This is also a pre-reading and visual literacy activity.

- How can you tell if a sign or poster is effective?
- What is the message? Is the message clear? Can you read it easily?
- What is a symbol?
- Do the other art elements—lines, shapes, and colors—add to or enhance the message? How?
- Do the art elements detract from the message? Why do you think so?

Activity 1

Planning the Wording

Motivation

Following a discussion of effective signs and posters, tell children that they will act as designers in order to advertise an area of the classroom or a special event. Discuss the purpose of the signs or posters that children will be creating.

Procedure

After children have decided on the message that they want to convey, brainstorm the words they could possibly use to get the message across. This is a good exercise to do as a class or in small groups.

- Have children figure out the fewest and most effective words to use on the sign or poster. Make sure they check the spelling.

- Allow children to practice sketching at least two possible layouts for the words on a piece of practice paper.
- Allow some time for children to practice working with the line printing tools to construct letters and words.

Take a few minutes to discuss the potential of the line tools by breaking down an interesting word into its components. As children make suggestions, demonstrate printing a word.

Activity 2

Planning the Layout

Motivation

Planning a sign or poster requires time and space for concentration and problem solving. Practice working with the paper space and the printing tools, without any ink, to figure out and adjust the position, placement, and spacing of letters and words.

Procedure

Have children follow these steps:

- Figure out the spacing (no ink).
- Try a practice print.
- Take a critical look at the practice print. Figure out how to correct mistakes.
- Make a final print.
- Add decorations and design elements that enhance the message.

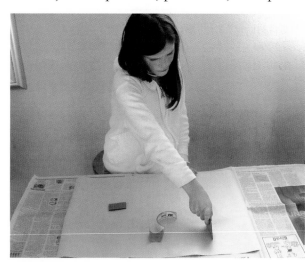

▶ video Watch a video of Olivia, age eight, planning the layout of her poster without ink.

54

Taking time to think and plan before beginning a task is a lifelong learning skill. In this case, a few minutes spent thinking and planning saves countless mistakes and a lot of paper. To facilitate planning and practicing, keep paint off of the table until you have seen children practice constructing and spacing letters and words. You might want children to show you their practice sketch before they begin.

Follow-up

Give children a second color to embellish their signs or posters. So that children focus first on the message, the lettering, and the layout, offer a second color to add interest only after the layout is complete.

Name sign by Keanu, age seven.

Olivia, age eight, with her finished poster.

"My name is a palindrome," says Hannah, age six.

Book   Klove, Lars. *I See A Sign*. New York: Aladdin Paperbacks, 1996.

Chapter 8
Snowflakes

Training the Hands, Eyes, and Mind

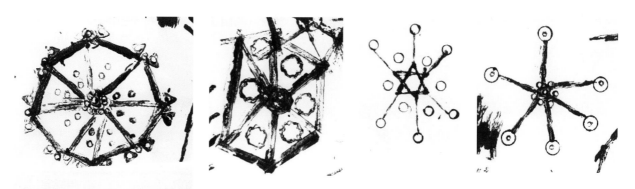

Details from a mural of snowflakes by first graders.

The crystalline structure of a snowflake is hexagonal (six-sided). The radiating design of each snowflake is unique. A study of snowflakes *expands upon radial design explorations in Part 1.*

Supplies

- large line tool to begin
- small line tool to add later
- 12" x 18" practice paper
- 12" x 18" blue paper
- white paint
- trays
- found objects

Learning Objectives
When students create snowflake designs they develop and practice
- strategies for creating a hexagon
- hand orientation, placement, and spatial skills
- using mathematical variables such as number, grouping, direction, alternation, position, length
- decorative design

 On the CD-ROM

Under SNOWFLAKES

Practicing
Printing

Solve a Geometry Problem

Motivation Solving the problem of how to construct a six-sided radial design can be an exciting challenge—especially on a snowy day. It is both a geometry problem and a design problem.

Procedure Ask students to think about ways to construct a hexagon using the straight line tools. Pick up on their ideas as you demonstrate a few strategies. Two suggestions are illustrated. Children will generate other solutions as they experiment.

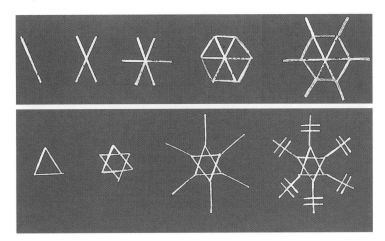

Print a diagonal line. Cross it. Cross it again. Embellish.

Print an equilateral triangle. Overlap with another equilateral triangle. Extend the points. Embellish. Can you come up with another way to construct a hexagon?

✳ Creating a clear beginning structure is the most difficult part of this project. Experiment first before trying this with children in order to see possibilities and to foresee problems.

Activity 1

Practice Constructing

Motivation Suggest that children begin by exploring strategies for constructing a hexagon and embellishing it on practice paper.

Procedure Offer only the large line tool to begin. Add the smaller tool when you observe that children need it.

Ask children to count the number of sides on their constructions. Often children create octagons instead of hexagons since they are easier to construct.

Watch a video of Ransom, age eight, carefully constructing the basic structure of his hexagon. He is just about to pick up the smaller line tool to create the sides of a hexagon.

▶ **video**

Activity 2
Printing

Hand out blue construction paper for children to create final prints. A new color paper can be a compelling stimulus to continuing working.

In this video clip you see Ransom, age eight, recreating his practice print and expanding the dimensions of his snowflake design. He now works faster and with greater confidence.

▶ video

Activity 3
Found Objects

Adding found objects to children's trays once they have a basic linear structure can be exciting. (See the "Suggestions for Supplies," at the beginning of this book, for examples of found objects.) However, found objects are not a necessity. Exquisite designs can be created with the large and small line tools. Sometimes these linear creations can be even more complex and interesting.

Once children have a basic structure, it is easy to embellish.

Follow-up

Have children try printing snowflakes of different sizes and add snowflakes or parts of snowflakes to their compositions. It is fine if some go off of the page. Snowflake designs can also be added to a large group mural.

Oil pastels create beautiful effects when added to compositions with white paint. Be sure that prints are dry before beginning.

This composition was created by a student teacher during an inservice workshop. Notice that she used only big and little lines.

Books

Martin, Jacqueline Briggs, and Mary Azarian. *Snowflake Bentley*. Boston: Houghton Mifflin, 1998.

Sugarman, Joan. *Snowflakes*. Boston: Little, Brown, 1985.

Wick, Walter. *A Drop of Water: A Book of Science and Wonder*. New York: Scholastic, 1997.

Chapter 9
Skeletons

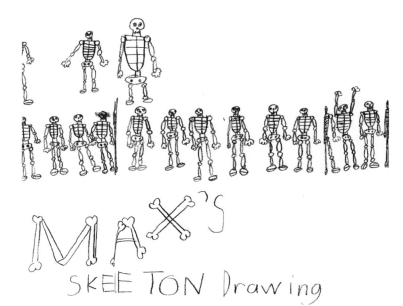

Max, age eight, drew this picture because he was intrigued by a photo of a skeleton that he saw in a book.

Although we may look different on the outside, on the inside we all have the same skeletal structure. The task of creating a skeleton causes children to take a closer look at the parts of the human body, the relationship of one body part to another, and at the many joints that allow the body to move.

Supplies

- large and small line tools
- the small curve
- 12" x 18" practice paper
- 12" x 18" black paper
- white paint
- trays
- photocopies of the skeleton on the following page

Learning Objectives
When students create skeletons they develop and practice

- hand orientation, placement, and spatial skills
- understandings about the human skeleton
- an awareness of the proportions and mechanics of the human body
- unique ways to use the line tools to create the bones that they need

 On the CD-ROM

Under SKELETONS

Anatomy
    Anatomy Exercises
    Parent Participation
Children's Strategies
Self-Assessment
Next Steps
Transforming Skeletons
Other Skeletons

Analyze the Anatomy of the Human Skeleton

Anatomy is the internal physical structure of an organism. Children will explore the skeletal structure of the human body.

Motivation

Begin by asking questions, such as, "What do you know about the human skeleton?" "What do you wonder about the human skeleton?" (Take notes as children respond.)

Share some interesting facts about the skeleton. For example,

- The skeleton is symmetrical.
- There are 206 bones in the human skeleton.
- There are 27 bones in each hand and 26 bones in each foot.
- More than half of the bones in the body are in the hands and feet!
- Anywhere that the body bends or moves, there is a joint.

✱ As with all other topics, a study of anatomy works best when it is part of a classroom investigation.

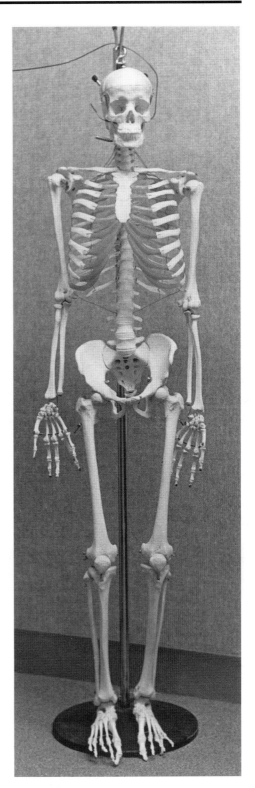

Activity 1

Drawing Bones

Motivation

Discuss strategies for printing different parts of the skeleton such as the rib cage, skull, pelvis, and hands and feet. Demonstrate strategies with the tools as children suggest them. Here are some sample discussion questions:

- What part of the skeleton will you print first? Why?
- How will you print the spine? the ribs? the joints?
- What problems do you anticipate? How will you solve them?

Marguerite, age ten, uses the line tools to recreate her understanding of the parts of a skeleton. Notice that she began with the skull.

Procedure

Practice using the line tools on practice paper to try out possibilities.

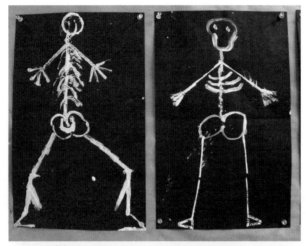

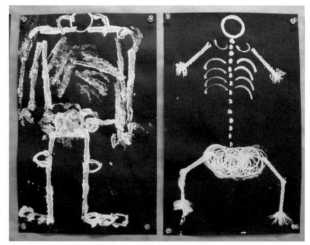

Skeletons printed by students in Bob Hepner's fourth-grade studio art class.

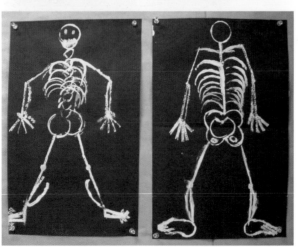

The teacher of these children suggested that they begin by printing the pelvis bone in the middle of their papers, working up to the skull and down through the legs to the feet. Some children followed this suggestion, whereas others had different strategies for beginning their skeletons. These children were fourth-graders who were studying the human body during a science unit.

It is especially important to take time to think about strategies and to practice possibilities before attempting to print complex structures like the skeleton.

Activity 2

Self-Assessment

Motivation   A great deal of learning can take place when children revisit their work. Both artists and scientists constantly revisit and refine their theories and their work. Pass out photocopies of the skeleton on page 61 for children to use to evaluate their practice skeletons before they print again. Repeating a challenging exercise such as this one is an invitation to observe more closely and to notice interesting subtleties that may have previously been overlooked.

Procedure   As children look at their prints, ask them to give feedback about what they learned from this activity.

- What did you know about the human skeleton?
- What did you learn?
- Are there any bones that you forgot?
- What will you do differently on your next print?

Let children know that it is okay to make mistakes. That is how we learn and that is why we take time to observe and practice. The goal isn't making a print with every bone in the body. The goal is to learn about the structure and function of the human skeleton.

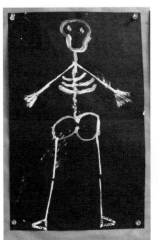

"Mine doesn't have a shoulder bone."

Activity 3

Skeletons in Action

After printing skeletons, children began to experiment with skeletons in action, enlargements of specific parts of the body, and animal skeletons. As we observe children, we can follow their lead and learn many ways to extend an exploration.

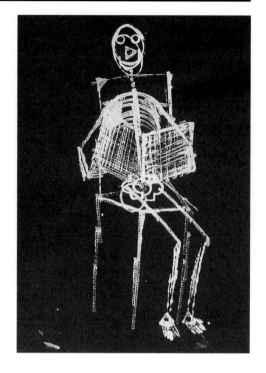

Sitting skeleton by Marguerite, age ten.

Follow-up

Transforming Skeletons with Oil Pastels

Practice prints and "mistakes" can be added to and transformed with oil pastels. In fact, this is a great way to use extra practice prints. The oil pastels glow when used over white paint and on dark paper. Children can think about other systems in the human body, or use their imaginations to create a character.

✱ Remember to place papers on a section of newspaper before adding color with oil pastels.

Shoshi, age ten, adds color to her practice print.

Books

Davidson, Sue, and Ben Morgan. *The Human Body Revealed*. New York: DK Publishing, Inc., 2002.

Livaudais, Madeleine, and Robert Dunne. *The Skeleton Book: An Inside Look at Animals*. New York: Walker & Company, 1972. (Note: Clear and bold black-and-white photographs of a variety of animals with concise descriptions.)

Chapter 10

Trees

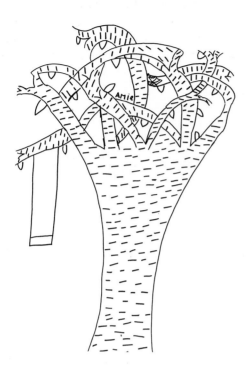

Trees are a common theme in children's representational drawings. Many children seem to have a favorite tree or a tree that is significant in their lives. The task of coming to know a tree by recreating it is a way to begin to form a relationship with the natural world and to appreciate the diversity within it. This same lesson could be adapted to the study of a variety of different types of plants.

Supplies

- large line tool to begin
- small line tool to add later
- practice paper 12" x 18"
- paper 12" x 18" or larger
- mural paper
- 1 color of paint
- trays
- pictures of trees that clearly show their branching structure

Learning Objectives

When students create trees, they develop and practice

- close observation of the natural world
- awareness of the beauty and complexity of structures in nature
- an understanding of branching structures (alternating, parallel, regular, irregular)
- an awareness of proportion and the relationships between tree parts (parts to whole)
- inventive ways of using the line printing tools

 On the CD-ROM

Under TREES

Observing Trees
Branching
Recreating Trees
Children's Strategies
Tree Mural
Related Projects
    Drawing Trees
    Leaf Rubbings

Observing Trees

Motivation   Analyze the structure of a few trees during a discussion.

Trees have characteristic branching patterns that become clear when we look at their silhouettes. We can easily pick out the pine, elm, and palm trees in the photographs shown here. However, linear structures in nature are more complex and often irregular. They are more difficult to observe and to recreate than human-made structures.

Pine tree.

Elm tree.

Palm tree.

Following the line structure of a particular tree is a way to observe and to recreate its distinctive way of branching. Deciduous trees are easiest to study in the fall, after they have lost their leaves.

Procedure   Point out interesting details about a particular tree and pose questions to help children focus their observations.

- Notice where the branches attach to the trunk of the tree.
- Notice that the branches become thinner and shorter as they move away from the trunk of the tree.
- Are the branches horizontal, vertical, or diagonal?
- Are they straight or curved?

✱ Young children often develop a way of drawing trees and other structures that they repeat over and over again. Studying a form, such as a particular tree, helps children expand their ways of working and thinking.

Activity 1

Branching Strategies

Motivation Introduce the printing tools and discuss strategies for creating branching structures. Ask, "If you were going to try to make this tree with line printings, how would you do it? Where would you begin?"

Procedure Demonstrate strategies as children suggest them. Three methods are adding on, leaving spaces, and the "V" method.

Adding on.
Print the vertical lines of the trunk. Add the branches.

Leave spaces.
Print the vertical lines of the trunk, leaving spaces where the branches will go.

The "V" method.
Print the vertical line of the trunk. Place a "V" where you want the trunk to branch.

These strategies came from observing groups of first- and second-graders using line printing to plan and print a mural of the forest.

Encourage children to try more than one strategy as they practice to see what works best for them. Support children who figure out alternative ways to create a branching structure.

Activity 2

Recreating Tree Structures

Motivation In order to recreate a particular kind of tree, one has to observe it closely and understand its characteristic structure. Display pictures of different kinds of trees for children to study.

Procedure Begin by having children observe and analyze the branching structure of a particular tree.

Then have them practice printing with the large line tool (no ink). Children should try out at least two of the three strategies (adding on, leaving spaces, or the "V" method).

Finally, have children print with paint.

Watch a video of the printing technique that Thea, age eight, discovered while printing her tree structure.

▶ video

Notice and share unique and unusual ways of using the line printing tools to create tree structures, needles, leaves, bark, and textures.

In order to encourage close observation, thinking, and experimentation, keep paint off of the table for a few minutes to allow time for children to test ideas. As you observe children testing strategies with the cardboard tool, place trays of paint on the table.

First graders involved in a study of the forest created a mural (details shown here) depicting the great variety of tree structures.

Books

Ehlert, Lois. *Red Leaf, Yellow Leaf*. San Diego: Harcourt Brace Jovanovich, 1991.

Locker, Thomas, and Candace Christiansen. *Sky Tree: Seeing Science Through Art*. New York: HarperCollins, 1995.

Robbins, Ken. *Autumn Leaves*. New York: Scholastic Press, 1998.

Chapter 11
Architecture

Orvieto, Italy. Photo by Diane Harr.

Blueprint by Kevin, age seven.

Architecture—the art and science of designing and erecting buildings—affects our lives more than any other type of art. Many of the architectural elements that we find in buildings and houses today come from *building traditions that are over 1,000 years old. The task of printing a structure that includes one or more architectural elements can awaken children's interest in architecture and history.*

Supplies

- large line tool to begin
- small line tool
- large and small curves
- 12" x 18" or larger practice paper
- 12" x 18" or larger paper
- 1 dark color of paint
- trays
- found objects, one per child
- pictures of built structures from the ancient world

Learning Objectives
When students create a building with architectural elements from ancient buildings, they develop and practice

- printing, planning, placement, construction, and designing skills
- observing and recognizing important architectural structures from different times and different parts of the world
- awareness of the built environment
- identifying architectural elements

On the CD-ROM

Under ARCHITECTURE

History
   Post & Beam
   Columns
   Greek Refinements
   Arch
   Dome
   Adaptations

Design a Building
   Plan and Practice
   Add a Curved Line
   Add Details
   Coloring In

Children's Strategies
   Parthenon
   Taj Mahal
   Caryatids
   Castles
   Animal Buildings
   Community Buildings
   Global Impact

Alternative Ideas
   Boats
   Monuments
   Parks

Related Projects
   A Treasure Hunt

An Abbreviated History of Architecture

Motivation

Spark interest in architecture by sharing an abbreviated history of architecture. We are fortunate that so many examples from the ancient world are still standing today.

Post and Beam

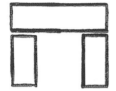

Stonehenge was built in England about 4,000 years ago. These enormous stones are one of the earliest examples that remain of post and beam construction.

Columns

The early Egyptians rounded the post to create the column. The ancient Greeks refined the column and, over a period of time, created three distinct new styles: Doric, Ionic, and Corinthian.

Doric: The simplest and heaviest of the columns.

Ionic: A much more graceful column. The capital (top of the column) is made up of two spirals called volutes.

Corinthian: The fanciest. Its capital is made up of small curling forms. Developed in the late, Greek Hellenistic period, this style was later very popular in Roman structures.

Greek Refinements: Entablature and Pediment

The ancient Greeks refined and lengthened the early post and beam construction. The posts became graceful columns. The beam became a rectangle filled with carvings and designs. The construction was able to support a triangular pediment which in turn supported a roof.

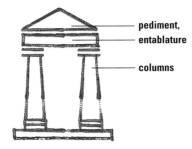

— pediment,
— entablature

— columns

Built 2,500 years ago on a hilltop in Athens, Greece, the **Parthenon** could be seen from all over the city. It was built to worship the goddess Athena and to hold the treasures of the city.

Arch

The Romans copied many Greek designs and added to them. Important additions were the rounded arch and the use of concrete, which opened up space and supported bigger and taller structures.

The **Pont du Gard,** in Nimes, France, was built by the Romans to carry water from high ground, across distances, to city reservoirs. Photo by Rose Leonard.

Dome

The invention of the arch led to the creation of the dome and the vaulted ceiling. These self-supporting structures opened up graceful overhead spaces more than ever before.

Dome of the Rock, 688 CE (Jerusalem).

Due to their ability to raise and open space without the need for central supporting pillars, domes and vaulted ceilings have been used in religious buildings worldwide to inspire awe and spirituality.

Each culture has changed and added to these basic forms.

The **Taj Mahal** in India was built in 1648 by Shah Jahan as a memorial to his wife. Notice the shape of the dome.

Activity 1

Design and Print a Structure Using Architectural Elements

Motivation   Tell children to pretend that they are architects and have been asked to design an important building for the community.

Procedure   Generate a list of community buildings with your students. Some suggestions by first- and second-graders include hospitals, libraries, sports stadiums, movie theaters, churches, synagogues, mosques, banks, and YMCAs. Children should include at least two architectural elements in their building designs. Provide them with these instructions:

1. Plan using the large cardboard (no paint).
2. Use practice paper to try out and print your beginning idea.
3. Add the other line tools.
4. Add found objects for decoration and details.
5. When you are ready, work on your final print. If you make a "mistake," figure out a way to use it to enhance your building.

▶ video   Watch a video of second graders beginning their buildings. Each child works in a very different way.

✱ Ask children to tell you what building they are planning to construct before dismissing them to their work areas. This ensures advanced planning and helps you spot those children who need a helping hand to get started. Always have a few extra pieces of paper available in case children really do need to start over.

Follow-up

Children begin with an idea that they clarify, refine, change, and expand upon as they work. Stories often develop in a parallel fashion as the children's work and their ideas grow in complexity. Older children can be encouraged to write a sentence, paragraph, or story about the idea behind their buildings. Guide children's writing with questions such as:

What gave you the idea?
How and where did you begin creating your structure?
Who lives or works in your building?

Books

Abhour, Marcy, with Rolaine Copeland Greta Greenberger. *Architecture in Education: A Resource of Imaginative Ideas and Tested Activities (K-12)*. Philadelphia: The Foundation for Architecture, 1986.

Caselli, Giovanni. *Wonders of the World*. New York: Dorling Kindersley, Inc., 1992.

Ceserani, Gian Paolo, and Piero Ventura. *Grand Constructions*. New York: G. P. Putnam's Sons, 1983.

D'Alelio, Jane. *I Know That Building*. The National Trust for Historic Preservation. Washington, D.C.: The Preservation Press, 1989.

Dutemple, Lesley A. *The Pantheon*. Minneapolis: Lerner Publications, 2003.

Isaacson, Philip M. *Round Buildings, Square Buildings, Buildings That Wiggle Like a Fish*. New York: Alfred A. Knopf, 1988.

Macaulay, David. *Castle*. Boston: Houghton Mifflin, 1977.

MacGregor, Anee, and Scott MacGregor. *Domes*. New York: Lothrop, Lee and Shepard, 1981.

Oxlade, Chris. *Bridges*. Austin, TX: Raintree Steck-Vaughn Publishers, 1997.

Paine, Roberta M. *Looking at Architecture*. New York: Lothrop, Lee and Shepard, 1974.

Severance, John B. *Skyscrapers: How America Grew Up*. New York: Holiday House, 2000. (Note: This is a history of skyscrapers and the architects who designed them. Geared to upper elementary children.)

Smith, A. G. *The American House: Styles of Architecture*. New York: Dover Publications, Inc., 1988. (Note: Officially labeled as a "coloring book" but contains simple line drawings of various types of homes.)

Chapter 12
Machines

Second graders studying "simple machines" during a science unit used line printing tools to practice creating levers, inclined planes, gears, wheels, and pulleys.

Star-making factory by Adrienne, age eight.

Supplies

- large and small line tools to begin
- the small curve, if needed
- found objects
- 12" x 18" practice paper
- 12" x 18" paper
- 1 color of paint
- trays

Learning Objectives
When students create simple and complex machines they develop and practice
- hand orientation, placement, and spatial skills
- understandings of simple machines
- awareness of different kinds of simple machines
- inventing ways to construct complex machines
- unique ways to use the line tools to create the parts that they need
- a beginning understanding of the conversion of energy through machines

 On the CD-ROM

Under OTHER TOPICS

Weather
Play Structures
Vehicles
Machines

76

Practicing Simple Machines

Motivation Identify, define, and discuss strategies for constructing simple machines using the line printing tools.

Procedure Children will use the line tools to print simple machines. Have them create at least two simple machines. Encourage them to try a lever, inclined plane, wedge, screw, wheel and axle, pulley, or gears.

Gears.

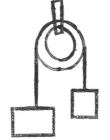

Pulley.

Wedge.

Invite children to share their strategies for creating each simple machine. Look especially for different ways to create the same kind of machine.

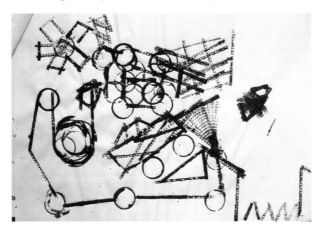

Practice print of a baseball factory by Eli, age eight.

Activity 1

Create a Complex Machine with Two or More "Simple Machines"

Motivation Brainstorm ideas for complex machines to create. Water transporter, cookie factory, and rock catapult were ideas suggested by a classroom of second-graders.

Procedure   Have children experiment on practice paper first.
Then, have children refine their ideas on a new sheet of paper.

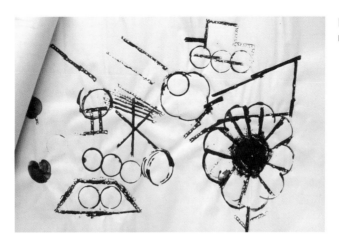

Practice print of simple
machines by Jefferson, age ten.

"The Crusher" by Jefferson, age ten.

Follow-up

Have children write a title and a paragraph about their machines, describing

- the simple machines within the construction
- the function of the machine
- how the machine works

Books   Bains, Rae. *Simple Machines*. Mahwah, NJ: Troll Associates, 1985.
Lampton, Christopher. *Sailboats, Flagpoles, Cranes: Using Pulleys as Simple Machines*. Brookfield, CT: Millbrook Press, 1991.
Rockwell, Anne F., and Harlow Rockwell. *Machines*. New York: MacMillan, 1972.

Bibliography

Arnheim, Rudolf. "Perceiving, Thinking, Forming," *Art Education: The Journal of the National Art Education Association*, March 1983.

Brosterman, Norman. *Inventing Kindergarten*. New York: Harry N. Abrams, 1997.

Edwards, Carolyn, et al. *The Hundred Languages of Children*, 2nd edition. Greenwich, CT: Ablex Publishing Corp., 1998.

Eisner, Elliot W. "What Do Children Learn When They Paint?" *Art Education: The Journal of The National Art Education Association*, 38, no. 3, March 1978.

Fletcher, Banister. *A History of Architecture on the Comparative Method*, 10th edition. New York: Charles Scribner's Sons, 1958. London: B.B. Batsford, Ltd., 1938.

Gandini, Lella. "Fundamentals of the Reggio Emilia Approach to Early Childhood Education," *Young Children: National Association for the Education of Young Children*, 41, no. 1, Nov. 1993.

Kellogg, Rhoda. *Analyzing Children's Art*. Palo Alto, CA: Mayfield Pub. Co., 1969.

Topal, Cathy Weisman. *Children, Clay and Sculpture*. Worcester, MA: Davis Publications, Inc., 1983.

———. *Children and Painting*. Worcester, MA: Davis Publications, Inc., 1983.

Topal, Cathy Weisman, and Lella Gandini. *Beautiful Stuff! Learning with Found Materials*. Worcester, MA: Davis Publications, Inc., 1999.

Townley, Mary Ross, in collaboration with Dorothy Dugdale. *Another Look*. Reading, MA: Addison-Wesley, 1978.

Appendix
Thinking with a Line and the National Standards

Content Standard 1: Understanding and applying media, techniques and processes

Benchmarks: Students describe how different materials, techniques and processes cause different responses. Students use different media, techniques, and processes to communicate ideas, experiences, and stories. Students use art materials and tools in a safe and responsible manner.

Lessons supporting this standard: 1–12

Content Standard 2: Using knowledge of structures and functions

Benchmarks: Students describe how different expressive features and organizational principles cause different responses. Students use visual structures and functions of art to communicate ideas.

Lessons supporting this standard: 6, 7, 11

Content Standard 3: Choosing and evaluating a range of subject matter symbols and ideas

Benchmarks: Students explore and understand prospective content for works of art. Students select and use subject matter, symbols and ideas to communicate meaning.

Lessons supporting this standard: 6–12

Content Standard 4: Understanding the visual arts in relation to history and culture

Benchmarks: Students identify specific works of art as belonging to particular cultures, times and places.

Lessons supporting this standard: 4, 6, 11

Content Standard 5: Reflecting upon and assessing the characteristics and merits of their work and the work of others

Lessons supporting this standard: 1–12

Content Standard 6: Making connections between visual arts and other disciplines

Lessons supporting this standard: 1–12

Principles and Standards for School Mathematics

Geometry Standard: Instructional programs from pre-kindergarten through grade 12 should enable all students to analyze characteristics and properties of two- and three-dimensional geometric shapes and develop mathematical arguments about geometric relationships.

Benchmarks:
- recognize, name, build, draw, compare and sort two- and three-dimensional shapes
- describe attributes and parts of two- and three-dimensional shapes
- classify two- and three-dimensional shapes according to their properties and develop definitions of classes of shapes such as triangles and pyramids.
- investigate, describe, and reason about the results of subdividing, combining and transforming shapes
- explore congruence and similarity
- create mental images of geometric shapes using spatial memory and spatial visualization
- recognize geometric shapes and structures in the environment and specify their location
- build and draw geometric objects
- recognize geometric ideas and relationships and apply them to other disciplines and to problems that arise in the classroom or in everyday life

Lessons supporting this standard: 2, 4, 5, 6, 8, 11, 12

National Science Education Standards

Life Science, Content Standard C: As a result of activities in grades K-4 all students should develop understanding of the characteristics of organisms.

Lessons supporting this standard: 8, 9, 10

Science and Technology Content Standard E: As a result of activities in grades K-4, all students should develop abilities to distinguish between natural objects and objects made by humans.

Lessons supporting this standard: 1, 2, 4, 5, 6, 8, 9, 10, 11, 12

English Language Arts Curriculum Framework General Standards

- Students will understand and acquire new vocabulary and use it correctly in reading and writing.

Chapters supporting this standard: 1–12

- Students will understand the nature of written English and the relationship of letters and spelling patterns to the sounds of speech.

Chapters supporting this standard: 3, 7

- Students will write with a clear focus, coherent organization and sufficient detail.

Chapters supporting this standard: 3, 7

- Students will write for different audiences and purposes.

Chapters supporting this standard: 7

Note: Thinking with a Line also supports early literacy standards.